Writing Lessons from the Front: Book 5

Evoking Emotion

Angela Hunt

Other Books in the Writing Lessons from the Front Series

The Plot Skeleton, Book 1

Creating Extraordinary Characters, Book 2

Point of View, Book 3

Track Down the Weasel Words, Book 4

Evoking Emotion, Book 5

Write Your Book: Plan and Process, Book 6

Hunt Haven
Press

Visit Angela Hunt's Web site at www.angelahuntbooks.com

ISBN: 0615848176
ISBN-13: 978-0615848174

"The novelist is like the conductor of an orchestra, his back to the audience, his face invisible, summoning the experience of music for the people he cannot see." – Sol Stein, *Stein On Writing*

1 THE ONE AND ONLY CHAPTER

I was a singer before I became a writer. I spent a year traveling throughout the United States as part of a ten-member vocal ensemble whose specialty was *a capella* arrangements and "God and Country" music.

Our director was and is a marvel—a great storyteller, an amazing musician, a teacher, a caring minister, and a disciplined mind. One day he said something I knew to be true: "It's all in the music," he said, talking about a wonderful arrangement of "God Bless America" we'd just rehearsed. "You can write in a standing ovation if you know what you're doing."

I listened in amazement. He was right; every time we sang "God Bless America" people rose to their feet at a certain point, applauding the entire time. How *did* he do it?

Years passed. I came off the road, got married, had children, raised a family and began to write. I learned about plotting, creating characters, and the art of revision. I studied every craft book I could find because I wanted my books to be the best they could be.

One day I was talking to a friend who ran a novelist's retreat where I often taught. I pointed out that I knew musicians who could write music that unfailingly evoked specific emotions and actions—so why couldn't we do the same thing in our writing?

"That sounds like a great class," she said. "Why don't you teach it?"

Gulp. I knew how to write scenes that moved my readers, but *how* did I do it? And how could I explain it to others?

For several days the question badgered me. I did an Internet search and found dozens of websites where writers were told to write "to evoke emotion," but I could not find much concrete advice on how to do that. Occasionally I found a page that reminded me to use details or music, description and memories, but those were things I used all the time. So how was I supposed to teach others how to evoke emotion?

Finally I turned my thoughts to what makes me cry. What moves *me*? And even though I am a rational, practical person at the core, I also feel deeply and can cry easily provided something moves me.

So what moves me? What makes me laugh? What makes me cry?

I came up with an answer in a flash: country music. Not those beer-drinkin', I-lost-my-cheatin'-lover kinds of songs, but the ballads that tell a story in three and a half minutes. Songs about old married couples and parents and kids, moms with prodigal daughters and dads raising hard-headed sons. Those kinds of songs.

I can't tell you how many times I've been driving down the road barely able to see because I've been bawling over some country song on the radio.

So why did those songs move me so much and so quickly?

I decided to analyze them, and in analyzing them I think I've come up with some common denominators we can translate into writing. So yes, we can write to deliberately evoke emotion. And while we may not make every reader cry, we can certainly touch their hearts and deepen the impact of our books. And isn't that what we want to do?

In his wonderful book *Stein on Writing*, Sol Stein says, ". . . the fiction writer's primary job . . . is creating an emotional experience for the reader."[1] E. L. Doctorow once wrote, "Good writing is supposed to evoke sensation in the reader, not the fact that it's raining, but the feeling of being rained upon."[2]

Our readers ought to be so submerged in our stories that they feel the wind on their faces, smell the fresh-cut grass, and shudder at the ominous sound of distant footsteps in the empty house. They are not supposed to see the writer at work, so it is our job to be invisible—just like an orchestra conductor at work.

The Key to Evoking Emotion

As I prepared my class on evoking emotion, I realized that the task boiled down to one simple principle: in order to evoke emotion in a limited amount of time and space, *you must tap into the well of emotion that already exists in the reader.*

In 1992, when Alexandra Ripley's *Scarlett* was released, I was among the thousands of readers who couldn't wait to read the official sequel to *Gone with the Wind.* I began to read only a few minutes after the book arrived at my house, and within a few pages I was sobbing . . . because Mammy died.

Was I sobbing because Alexandra Ripley made Mammy seem so appealing and wonderful that I fell in love with her within the space of a few pages? With no disrespect intended for Ms. Ripley, no. I wept because I had fallen in love with Mammy in Margaret Mitchell's *Gone with the Wind.* Mammy and I had bonded in the many times I read GWTW, and when she died in *Scarlett,* I cried as though I had lost a real friend.

Alexandra Ripley didn't lay the emotional groundwork for my tears; Margaret Mitchell did. But Ms. Ripley was smart enough to tap into what Mitchell had established and keep me reading the rest of her book.

That is our task as writers. We have to keep our reader in mind and try to think of the emotional situations in their lives. How can we tap into those feelings and memories? To do this, we have to be aware of the culture our readers live in, and we have to be willing to lay bare our own emotional histories. I've had personal and family traumas of my own, and whenever a reader says, "I could tell you've been through something just like the story in your book," I know I've done my job.

This May be Unusual, But . . .

As much as I appreciate the writer's art, I also realize that a picture—especially a *moving* picture—is worth a thousand words. So I would like you to watch a few videos as you study this writing lesson. You can move on without watching the videos, of course, but you'll get much more out of this lesson if you participate fully—and that means sitting back and watching a few YouTube vids. (Of course, if you're reading the e-book version of this lesson and have access to wi-fi, this will be easy.)

Ready? We're about to get interactive.

If you haven't seen Beyonce's version of "Single Ladies," take a few seconds to look at this. You don't have to watch the entire thing. Just a couple of seconds will do, enough to get the general idea. (If the link doesn't work, search for *Beyonce Single Ladies* on youtube.com.)

http://www.youtube.com/watch?v=eREH27Zc7NY

Got the idea? Okay—now look at this parody of "Single Ladies." And *do* watch all of this one. (If the link doesn't work, search for *wrinkled ladies* on youtube.com.)

http://www.youtube.com/watch?v=NCvHgppVey4

What did you think? Did you smile? I love Anita Renfroe's version; I love the look, the moves, and that bit about growing wrinkles of our own . . .

Part of my laughter, of course, comes from the fact that I'm over fifty and I relate personally to everything Anita sang. In fact, at this stage of my life, I relate a lot more to Anita than to Beyonce. Maybe you do, too.

What, specifically, did we find funny about the wrinkled ladies?

First, it was a parody. Exactly like the Beyonce video, and yet nothing like it.

Second, humor always contains an element of truth, and the wrinkled ladies song was truth exaggerated. Yes, we're all going to wrinkle eventually, but we're not going to dance around in leotards in celebration of that fact.

Third, those ladies were celebrating themselves in an unusual way. We laughed, but we laughed *with* them, not *at* them. Most of us who are of a certain age were thinking we'd fit right in if we were dancing on that soundstage.

Fourth—humor usually contains an element of the unexpected. Most people try to hide their wrinkles and their no-longer-slim bodies, yet those women were celebrating every bulge and bump and asking for a "bowl of sugar, put some cream on it, don't be mad when you see your skin don't fit." I love it!

When considering how to put a program together, I have learned that laughter is the key that unlocks a listener's—or a reader's—heart. People have walls around their hearts, most folks tend to be guarded. If we want to reach inside their hearts and get through the wall, laughter is the way to do it.

So one of the first emotions you need to evoke in your book or story is humor. Find a place—preferably up front—where you can make your reader laugh or smile.

"But it's a murder mystery," you may be muttering. "People are dying all over the place."

People were dying all over the place in *Jaws*, too, but Spielberg remembered to add humor. Sheriff Brody was always joking—with a straight face—that they needed a bigger boat. That oft-repeated line broke the tension and made it possible for audiences to sit through the tension and the gore of violent shark attacks.

When I was planning to write my Fairlawn series, about a woman who inherits a funeral home, I knew I'd have to overcome a certain "ick" factor. So I gave my protagonist a full dose of the heebie jeebies and made her squeamish about the operations of a funeral home. This enabled me to ease my protagonist—and my reader—into the funeral industry, gently explaining why it's important, how the work is accomplished, and how it can be considered a ministry and not a gruesome job. By the end of the third book, Jennifer is a mortician herself.

I also made certain that for every grim story line, I had an equally humorous storyline. In one book a woman has a "Red Hat" funeral, complete with kazoos, and in another book a woman plans a fake funeral so she can lie in the coffin and hear what her friends really think about her.

Humor is important. So plan on including something to make your reader chuckle.

Maybe you need to add another character to your story, a small child or a quirky maiden aunt, who can be the focus of a humorous storyline. Or maybe you need to heighten your protagonist's sense of humor. The next time you read a book or watch a movie, look for the funny bits and notice where they are placed. They're present for a reason—to break the tension and make the reader/viewer smile.

Now we're going to look at a second video: "God Bless America," the arrangement I mentioned earlier. You'll probably be listening alone, so you're not likely to stand up and cheer, but see if you can determine the point where audiences always rose to their feet—and why. (If the link doesn't work, search for *Re'Generation: God Bless America* on youtube.com).

Here's the link:
http://www.youtube.com/watch?v=LvRt6I6Do0w

Did you watch all of the video? How did it move you? Let's analyze why.

We saw beautiful images of people and places we could all identify or identify *with*: small children, grandparents, little babies, nonconformist teens. We saw the central prairies, the rocky western coast, southern live oaks, and the rugged northeastern coasts. We saw Chinatown in D.C., several Washington memorials, quiet forests and high-tech highways. We had humor—adorable tiny ballerinas and a boy praying with his dog. We saw our men in military uniform and war memorials for those who did not come home alive. The tones of the images—majestic, cute, beautiful, pastoral—varied as well. Surely some of those images touched all of us in some way.

We also felt the appeal of patriotism. Those of us who love this country for its ideals felt a tug at our heartstrings—we *do* beg God to bless America, to forgive her failures and bless her for her attempts to do good. We were also moved by the beauty of a well-know and well-beloved song. "God Bless America" isn't our national anthem, but the song is a national favorite.

Those elements can translate into words, more or less. We can describe warriors and pioneers and community leaders. We can transport our characters to beautiful landscapes and historic monuments and fill them with the spirit of patriotism.

But let's look at the musical devices the song used to create an effects. First, the volume—sections of the song were *forte*, very loud, with singers at full volume and trumpets trumpeting. Other sections were *a capella* and actually spoken in whispers: the prayers of "God bless America."

Did you find the place where audiences always rose to their feet? The standing ovation always occurred near the end, as the key change led into a chorus of "America the Beautiful." That key change literally lifted people out of their chairs because they were carried along by music which moved *upward*.

Can we translate musical volume and key changes into written words? More on that topic later.

For now, let's look at another video. (If the link doesn't work, search for *Christian the Lion I will always love you* on youtube.com.)

http://www.youtube.com/watch?v=KCb64TjNZ54

I don't know about you, but I can be feeling as dry as a milk bucket under a bull until this video plays. Then the waterworks start and I can't stop them.

Part of this video's effectiveness, of course, lies in the song. There are several other vids about Christian the Lion on YouTube, and they're not nearly as effective because the song doesn't work as well as "I Will Always Love You." And we can't ignore that poignant pause—total silence for a couple of beats as the lion looks at the two men and then charges. Will he attack them? No— he hugs them! Our tension and nervous anticipation is rewarded many times over as the lion frolics and displays his obvious affection for the two men he knew as a cub.

We love this video for many reasons. First, it demonstrates that animals have memories and form real bonds with their humans. (Score one for the animal lovers!) Second, seeing real love and joy and delight uplifts the viewer. We want to rejoice with those who rejoice, so seeing this joyful reunion lifts our spirits. Third, we have a clear sense that we are seeing selfless love. Animals have no ulterior motives (or not in this case, anyway). The lion isn't being affectionate to get a treat. He's running toward the men because he's happy to see them and because he has bonded to them them. Isn't that what love is?

As a Christian, I find this video moving for two additional reasons. It reminds me of the biblical promise that one day in the future, the lion will lay down with the lamb. Animals will no longer hunt and kill each other, and the natural fear they feel toward man will be erased.

And how can anyone who's familiar with C.S. Lewis's parables look at a lion and not think of Aslan, the powerful and loving lion who symbolizes Christ? This video not only comforts and delights me in the present, but it reminds me of the future and makes me homesick for heaven.

How can these things be translated into written words? Think about the themes—love, joy, selfless giving. We are moved when we see these ideals portrayed in scenes, whether they're in films or novels. As our society grows darker and more selfish, stories of strangers who sacrifice for another person grow more rare. I get teary-eyed when I read newspaper accounts of firemen who help free kittens from sewer drains, or businessmen who stop traffic so a mother duck and her babies can cross a highway. We *hunger* for stories about virtuous acts.

What do we see on TV? What genres are top-sellers in our bookstores? Crime stories, murder mysteries, horror films. We are surrounded by darkness in reality and our entertainment, so it's no wonder that our spirits lift when we encounter a rare moment of goodness.

I can hear some of you sputtering now. You don't want to write a saccharine story that's all sweetness and light. You want your books to feel real and gritty, populated by characters who face real problems.

That's fine. But remember the power of the positive moment. The darker your story world is, the brighter the light shining in it.

This next video is a fun family romp, but it teaches us a lot about what moves people. (If the link below doesn't work, search for *Rodney Atkins Watching You* on youtube.com).

http://www.youtube.com/watch?v=oqYUns2YQik

I particularly like this video because it's upbeat—proving that you can elicit emotion without getting maudlin about it. What did you find moving?

The first thing I notice is the simple power of story. This is a complete story with a beginning, middle, and ending. The dad sees his kid do something, realizes that the child is imitating what he's seen Daddy do, and then the father prays to ask for help and forgiveness. Later that night, when the little buckaroo prays on his own, Dad realizes that maybe he's doing some things right.

Delightful lesson learned in a positive way, and a welcome reminder that our children are always watching us.

Did you notice the use of humor? The video is filled with images to make people smile—the boy and his dad clowning around on the porch, the kid making faces at the camera, the boy wagging his finger as the father does the same thing to his child. Humor, right at the start and throughout the video.

How did the video make this lesson pertain to almost every adult who watches it? I saw dozens of items common to most American homes: the wall marked with lines to indicate a child's growth, pictures held up by magnets on the refrigerator door, the mention of happy meals and chicken nuggets. How many of us have or have had those things in our homes? The sight of these common elements helps the viewer tap into his or her own emotional well, so the video grabs us almost immediately.

And how many of us who are parents haven't had a moment when we regretted saying or doing something in front of our child? The songwriter tapped into something else we've all experienced: parental guilt. We know what we ought to do, but so many times we fall short. We want to be good parents, but we're human and we make mistakes. I believe every parent has felt the pang of remorse at least once in his parenting career. The feeling is particularly acute when it's our child who points out our mistake, as in this video.

But perhaps the most moving force in this short clip is the simple portrayal of the love between a father and his son. We see love in their hugs, smiles, and joking around. And if we have felt that kind of love at any point in our lives, we will look back, remember, and feel the same thing. And that's a beautiful illustration of how the songwriter evoked emotion by tapping into the viewer's own emotional well.

One more video, and then we'll get to the application of these insights. If the link below doesn't work, search for *Brad Paisley He Didn't Have to Be* on youtube.com.

You might want to have a couple of tissues handy.

http://www.youtube.com/watch?v=BjO1F6oCab8

Excuse me while I blow my nose. There. That particular video gets me every time. Why?

Once again, we're told a story with a beginning, middle, and end. Unfortunately, it's a familiar story about a fatherless boy who feels abandoned—that is, until a wonderful man falls in love with his mother and wants to include him in the new family. The boy moves from abandonment to acceptance, and once again we rejoice in a bright moment of goodness in a sad situation.

I particularly appreciate that love is beautifully depicted without once being mentioned. He doesn't sing about love, love, love, but you see it in every frame of the film and every line of the song. Talk about showing and not telling!

In quick clips we see photos of the family together, the step-dad teaching the boy how to throw and hit a ball and how to ride a bike, and we glimpse all the memories of growing up with a loving dad. Those of us who had similar childhoods will be moved by the memory of our fathers, and those who didn't have a loving father may feel a longing for something they never had.

I think all parents remember how helpless and insecure we felt when someone placed a new baby into our arms. We had no idea what the future would hold, and somewhere in the back of our minds we may have worried that we would mess up this tiny human being. We felt vulnerable and helpless to a degree, yet this man looks to the man standing beside him—the man who didn't have to be his father, but chose to be.

Keep Your Reader in Mind

A few years ago I taught a writing course at Taylor University. When I taught this material, I showed the same videos I've featured here . . . and noticed something. A few of my students were visibly moved at the Christian the Lion clip, but few of them had any emotional reaction to the later videos.

Why? I had to smile when the answer struck me. Most of them were young people in their late teens or early twenties, and they'd had pets, so they related to the love between the lion and the two Englishmen. But only a couple of the older students were parents, so the majority of them simply watched the family-centered videos and smiled.

They had no emotional memories of having a baby . . . raising a child . . . or making a mistake as a parent. I learned a lesson in that class—when writing an emotional scene, keep the emotional experiences of your most likely reader firmly in mind.

We've Identified the Elements—How Do They Translate to Writing?

How can we create beautiful music in our written scenes? How can we create dramatic, poignant pauses like the one in "Christian the Lion?"

How do we raise and lower the volume of a scene? How do we "change keys" or move from a full orchestra to a whisper?

How do we portray emotion without getting sappy about it? How do we portray a noble value like love, self-sacrifice, loyalty, joy, or goodness in a way that's believable and real?

Most important, how do we identify and tap into the well of

emotion within our readers?

(When I teach this lesson at workshops, I analyze passages from other novelists, but here I'll use excerpts from my own work so I won't have to deal with copyright and permissions issues. I hope you will excuse what must look like flagrant self-promotion.)

My novel, *Unspoken*, features a protagonist, Glee, and my favorite character: Sema, a gorilla. Glee has raised Sema since the gorilla's infancy and considers the animal her child. Furthermore, Glee has taught Sema sign language, so the gorilla communicates with her. Sema has a personality all her own—she loves Glee, she hates all species of cats, and she is not above name-calling when the mood suits her.

Not only is Sema occasionally funny (Stinky nut! Is one of her favorite exclamations), but I inserted humor into the book after a particularly tense scene where Sema drowns in the moat around the zoo's gorilla enclosure and is then resuscitated. After her near death experience, Sema begins to sign about a "shiny man" she sees. Not seeing any "shiny man," Glee is convinced that Sema suffered brain damage while she was deprived of oxygen, so she and a friend sneak Sema out of the zoo and into a clinic for an MRI.

Later, Glee reluctantly leads Sema to a public pavilion where she is to "perform" for a group of visitors to the zoo. I have inserted brackets to make note of elements that heighten the emotion. (You might want to read this twice, ignoring the bracketed information the first time, and studying it the second.)

As soon as we moved from the exit and into the sun, Sema straightened and walked bipedally, **slipping her hand into mine. [Any parent who has ever walked hand in hand with her child will identify with this.]** The gesture caught me by surprise—as eager as she was, I had expected her to practically pull me down the path. But perhaps this excursion frightened her—after all, the last time she ventured into the depths of the zoo, she'd been drowning.

We strolled beneath the sprawling limbs of a live oak, lacy with gilded spring leaves. The asphalt path baked in a golden sunshine that hinted of a warmer afternoon to come. **[Notice that the**

15

scene begins on a quiet note, with leisurely descriptive sentences.]

On Sunday mornings, when the only individuals stirring were khaki-clothed employees and animals, Thousand Oaks seemed a welcoming place. Whenever Sema saw something interesting, she stopped on the path and sank to a squatting position as her hands flew in various questions.

Her curiosity didn't surprise me. Though she had glimpsed all sorts of situations through television and travel in my car, she had never seen so many wheeled refreshment stands, souvenir kiosks, and symbols. A sign stood at each intersection along our path, and cartoon images of animals adorned each wooden marker. Sema wanted to know about every species. [Again, any parent who has ever patiently answered their child's questions will identify.]

She pointed to a picture of a pink flamingo. *Lip stick bird?*

I laughed. "He is the color of lipstick, isn't he? And he has long legs. He's called—" I hesitated, not knowing the sign for *flamingo*. "Well, we'll find the sign later."

She pointed to a picture of a wombat, one of the most popular animals in the Australian Outback exhibit. *Fur pig?* [Little bits of humor are inserted here as preparation for the drama that lies ahead.]

"Um, I think that's a . . ." I paused to think of a sign, then combined a *W* with the sign for *pig*, hand beneath the chin with flapping fingers. "Wombat." Any marsupial expert would chastise me for implying that wombats and pigs were related, but Sema had made the connection, not me.

The wind picked up, sending a wave of oak leaves toward us with a sound like scattering seashells. [The wind is picking up—mood music to indicate the approach of something

ominous. Similar to a faster tempo in music.]
I glanced at the sky, knowing that spring winds
often brought sudden showers. A cloudbank had
risen behind the crest of the oak behind us and
the air had become thick and damp. **[More mood
music to establish an increasingly threatening
atmosphere despite the light conversation
they're having.]**

"Come on, sweetie, we need to move on.
Remember my surprise? We're almost there."
**[Glee's use of endearments reminds readers of
their children.]**

Glee give toy?

"Not a toy, my girl, something else. I'll explain
after we look at a few books."

Obediently, Sema took my outstretched hand.
We continued our steady walk along the path that
led to the amphitheater where local high school
bands played on Saturday afternoons and the
community college chorale sang on summer
nights. How many guests would the amphitheater
hold, two hundred? Since Matthews had insisted
on this location, he must be expecting a crowd.

I looked around. In the distance, a custodian
pushed a wheeled garbage can toward one of the
brick restrooms while a hungry sea gull hovered
above the man's head, probably hoping for a
scrap. The custodian hadn't noticed us, and I
didn't want to attract his attention. Better to get
Sema calmly situated backstage before anyone else
began to mill about.

Aware of the passing time, I tugged on Sema's
arm, urging her forward. She walked slowly,
rocking on her hips, her head swiveling to check
out sights and sounds she'd never had an
opportunity to investigate. A flock of sparrows
moved as one over our heads, then looped back to
settle on the branches of an oak ahead of us.

"Look there." I pointed toward the birds. "All
those little friends have come to say hello."

Without warning, the stillness of the setting shivered into bits, the echoes of a siren scattering the sparrows. Sema's fingers tightened around mine as I looked around. What was this, a fire drill? **[Like any alarmed parent, Glee is thinking of her charge—and the scattering sparrows reinforce the idea that she needs to flee.]**

I searched the sky and saw no signs of smoke, but the wail continued, lancing the silence, drilling straight into my head. "Come on, Sema." I tugged her toward the amphitheater. "We need to hurry."

She jerked her hand from mine. Amazed at this unexpected display of rebellion, **[another phrase that will remind parents of a similar situation in their lives]** I turned, a rebuke on my tongue, and saw the white tiger crouching beside an overturned garbage can no more than twenty feet away. The cat lay flat against the asphalt, his hindquarters twitching, his golden eyes focused on us. Sema uttered no sound at all, but the rank odor of fear rose from her glands and invaded my nostrils. **[Sensory details—in this case, the sense of smell—heightens emotional involvement in the scene.]**

What should we do? Some rational part of my brain, the small portion not occupied with immediate panic, told me to face the creature and wave my arms in an effort to make myself look bigger and more intimidating, but who could listen to reason when faced with a man-eater? Instinct screamed *run!*, but I couldn't run. I had to think of Sema, whose African cousins occasionally faced leopards. According to gorilla researchers, *sometimes* the gorilla won the encounter—

[Long run-on sentences stretch out the story moment and give us access to Glee's frantic thoughts. Anyone who has ever been in a similar frightening situation will relate to this.]

But tigers were four times heavier and stronger than leopards, and Sema had not been reared in the wild. Neither did she like cats, not even Nana's calico.

"Sema." I struggled to push words past the lump of ice in my throat. "Sweetie, don't move." **[Sensory detail—cold ice in her throat, coupled with another endearment for Sema.]**

The wind pushed at my hair, bringing with it the sound of cars on the highway. Hard to believe civilization and salvation lay a few feet away and we were standing in one of the nation's most cosmopolitan areas— **[When faced with panic, some part of the brain does keep ticking off odd little details . . .]**

The tiger's whiskers quivered with the ghost of a growl. The low sound scraped across my nerves, but as long as he didn't charge, we might be able to escape. **[More mood music. The sound scraping across her nerves could well be the scrape of a bow across a cello . . .]**

I glanced toward the restroom, where the custodian had disappeared. If I screamed, he would come running. He carried a radio, all the maintenance crew did, and he would call for help. In the worst case scenario, I might have to wrestle with the tiger, but if I screamed loud enough, the animal might run away.

"Sema," I strengthened my voice and slipped the loop of her leash from my wrist, "see the big tree ahead of us? I want you to run to the tree. Run as fast as you can, okay? Climb up in the tree and don't come down until you see Brad."

I wasn't sure she understood until she released my hand. I looked down, grateful that my words had taken hold, but Sema only lifted her arms and pulled the bent fingers of both hands across her face. In a barely comprehendible flash I realized she was signing *tiger*. But this wasn't the cuddly tiger of her Winnie the Pooh book; this one could kill us. [Any parent or child who has read Winnie the Pool will relate.]

I ignored her sign. "Ready to run, Sema? Okay—*go!*"

The tiger charged at the sound of my shout. I pushed at Sema's shoulder, thinking she would run to the tree while I waved my arms and drew the cat's attention, but Sema, my brave girl, ran straight toward the beast. [*My brave girl*—making Sema human makes her seem like the reader's daughter as well.]

I froze as terror lodged in my throat, making it impossible to utter another cry. The heavy air filled with the shrill sounds of screams and snarls as the tiger took Sema down. My sweet girl exhibited traits I'd never seen in her, flashing her canines as she roared. The powerful stink of fear blew over me as the two combatants rolled on the thin grass, teeth flashing, claws ripping, blood flowing. [This scene began on a quiet note, but the crescendo has brought us to a loud battle. Notice the insertion of smells, sounds, and sights.]

The world had shrunk to a black and white blur when I heard sharp sounds, one shot followed by another. The tiger roared again, then collapsed. Sema rose unsteadily to a standing position, looked at me, then folded gently at the knees and toppled backward. [The loud, frantic fight is over, interrupted by the crack of a gun. And suddenly . . . silence.]

Both animals lay on the grass beside the path. The tiger's side rose and fell in one last shudder. Sema lay flat, her eyes wide, her gaze focused on the spreading limbs of the treetop canopy overhead. [We are quiet again, more references to the peaceful trees that were mentioned at the beginning of the scene. But the situation has changed.]

"Sema!" I sank to the ground and frantically

ran my hands over her torso. [**Every parent who has ever had a child suffer injury will remember this feeling.**] Had she been shot, too? My palm came away wet and red when I brushed her chest; gouts of blood pumped from a gash on her neck. She might have wounds on her back as well, but I didn't want to move her until help arrived.

"Help!" I couldn't seem to draw in enough air to push a shout out of my throat. "Could someone please help me?" [**When the worst happens, life seems to stop.**]

From somewhere to my right a pair of men ran forward, but I dared not take my eyes off Sema for more than an instant. Her hands rose as though she wanted to say something, but I shook my head.

"Be still, Sema, until help comes. Someone will be here in a minute. You know how I've always taught you to be patient?" My voice cracked. "You need to be patient now." [**Note the physical details—voice cracking, pretending to be brave and confident.**]

Love shone in her eyes as her face settled into lines of contentment. Such emotions are difficult for humans to falsify; I now believe it is impossible for animals to lie about love.

Her hands rose again. *Sema go.*

"Sure, sweetie, we're going home in a few days. We'll be back in the trailer before you know it, and I'm going to take care of you until you feel better. We'll be able to read and play and watch movies—"

Shiny man say . . . her hands faltered . . . *Sema go now.*

"No, Sema, not now, don't do this. You don't have to go anywhere. You stay with me, stay here, so I can take care of you. Don't you even think about leaving, girlie, because Brad's going to help me take care of you and I know you like Brad.

Together we're going to make sure nothing like this ever happens again—" **[Glee's sentences grow choppier as her panic rises. She's rambling and she knows it, but she'll do or say anything to stave off what she fears most.]**

Sema happy. Sema love.

Her head lolled to the right and the spark of life slipped from her eyes. Emptiness rushed in to fill her face and I didn't need a doctor to tell me her heart had stopped. **[More physical details.]**

Swallowing the sob that rose in my throat, I pulled her closer, pillowing her head in my lap. In that moment I understood the mystifying behavior of elephants and gorillas that lose loved ones—I wanted to pound on her chest, slap the dullness from her eyes, do anything I could to catch the spirit of life and force it back into her body.

But it had gone. I sat on the grass, numb to everything, as color ran out of the world and the clouds began to weep. **[The scene ends on another quiet note, accompanied by the "mood music" of a quiet sky weeping in consolation.]** [3]

Do you see how you can cobble the things we've discovered into a scene? You can vary the volume by moving from slow-paced passages to faster-paced events. You can change the tempo by varying sentence and word length. You can add mood music to enhance whatever you're describing. And, perhaps most important, you can tap into your reader's emotional memories by writing about things they've thought, said, and done.

Did you notice that Glee did not weep in the scene above? The clouds did, but nowhere did I mention Glee weeping. I could have written *I sat on the grass and sobbed,* but that would have been too "on the nose." Much better to pull back and let the world weep for Glee and Sema.

A actor friend of mine once explained a dramatic trick that works well in fiction. "Sometimes," he said, "an actor will noticeably choke back tears . . . and the audience will feel compelled to supply the emotion the actor is repressing." So if you want your reader to feel grief or hilarity or anger, have your character struggle to rein in his grief or his laughter or his urge to knock someone's block off. The reader will then feel the emotion your character is struggling to restrain. In the scene above, Glee does not weep, but the clouds do, and so will the reader . . . I hope.

Here's another scene, this one from *The Fine Art of Insincerity*, featuring another emotion revealed only through interior monologue. I've condensed it a bit.

> There's a baby.
>
> My husband is having a baby. With another woman. A difficult situation involving one interloper has become an impossible situation involving two. **[Notice the short sentences and sentence fragments. She is angry, so long, flowing sentences wouldn't have matched her mindset.]**
>
> Michael's latest confession has left me anxious and bewildered, too agitated to sleep. I'm still awake when I finally hear the front door close, followed by the roar of a car engine and the pop of tires over gravel. I'd heard voices from downstairs, so one of my sisters must have talked to Michael before he left. I can't imagine what was said. **[Notice the physical details—specific sounds. When a scene is mostly internal, you need external details to keep it anchored.]**
>
> I hope he thinks about what he's done to our family on the drive home.
>
> Still . . . in the solitude of my room I have to admit I had hoped Michael would say something that would help me make sense of this situation. **[Now she's calming down, so the sentences lengthen and begin to flow.]** At first I'd clung to the hope that he'd tell me the woman was going through a divorce of her own, so he'd been a friend and counselor, nothing more. But he and this woman have created a baby . . . and, knowing Michael, he will want to do the best thing

for all concerned. Which leaves me to do . . . what, exactly? **[Notice the use of ellipses. These create a pause in the flow of interior monologue, allowing her comments to feel more natural and thoughtful.]**

I lie in the darkness, staring at the moonlit walls while my imagination cobbles together possible outcomes: obviously, I could divorce him, release him to marry his lover and be a father to her child. I would be left alone and our sons would lose a lot of respect for their father. They're old enough to understand what Michael did, and they might not want to forgive him. **[Clearly, this woman is more thinker than feeler, but she's still feeling plenty. But the practical side of her nature is planning for the future. Your reader has probably had nights where she lay awake in bed and thought about her marriage or her children. Anyone who has ever passed a sleepless night will relate to this.]**

. . . A blush burns my cheek. How tawdry it all is! The story will spread around the college, our neighborhood, our church. People who love Michael might hear the rumor and grant him the benefit of the doubt, but the baby will be proof of his guilt. And as our friends whisper over dinner tables and cell phones, people will speculate about what I might have done to drive him away. Did I neglect him? Was I frigid or overbearing? People who know me will assume it's all my fault, that my organization and list-making drove bookish Michael straight into another woman's arms. What they don't know is that Michael *appreciates* my organization skills—they're responsible for keeping our family stable.

I don't think I did anything to drive Michael away, but my opinion doesn't matter. People will talk. The only way I can preserve my reputation is to remain steady and behave as normally as possible. Since I didn't cheat, why should I suffer?

Nothing about this is fair.

Perhaps I shouldn't surrender the high ground. Michael's the one who strayed, so he should be the one to leave the house. But when should he leave? If I tell him to leave until we settle the situation, where will he go if not to the other woman? And once he's ensconced in her house or apartment, how am I to get him back . . . if I *want* him back? Do I? Do I want him at all?

Right now I can't imagine ever wanting him again. My brain, which has always benefited from a fertile imagination, is supplying me with all sorts of unpleasant mental images: Michael walking with a leggy young professor on campus, driving her home in his car, entering her apartment, falling into her bed. It takes no effort to imagine him in her arms, skin against skin, to hear the endearments he might have whispered in her ear. **[What wronged wife hasn't imagined the physical details of an affair? And rare is the reader who doesn't care what people think.]**

I grit my teeth and roll over to face the wall, dropping the curtain on my dark visions. My husband has been with another woman. Why? Was I not enough for him? Am I no longer attractive? I'm not the waif he married, but I've borne him two children. I've stood by Michael's side for twenty-seven years, fretting with him over employment cuts at the college and family financial crises. I've stayed up with him while we struggled to figure out how we were going to finance two boys in college. I've spent a half dozen nights in a hospital easy chair, watching over Michael's son as he recovered from an emergency appendectomy. I've put miles on this body for Michael and his children, and I've done my best to hold back the ravages of time. **[What woman hasn't doubted her beauty? We may**

pretend that we don't care about aging, but we do. Any woman over forty will relate to Ginger's thoughts.]

Obviously, I didn't do enough. I faced a competitor I didn't even know existed, but now she's standing between me and my husband, between Michael and our sons. She's bringing a new life into the world, a life Michael will be responsible for—

I groan at the thought of adding child support payments to an already-stretched budget. And college! And orthodontia and education expenses and a regular allowance—all the things children want and need. If Michael sets up his own place, he will not only have to pay for an apartment and utilities, but he will have to pay child support to the other woman. He might be forced to move into her apartment simply for financial reasons.

Yet the alternative is inconceivable. How can I stay with a man who betrayed me? Whose actions will tell the world that I didn't satisfy his needs? Staying with Michael might mean I would be forced to endure this woman's child in my home on weekends, summers, and alternate holidays. I would have to open my heart and life to the child of a woman who stole what belonged to me, the right to enjoy my husband's body. The right to occupy first priority in his heart. **[The intact, two-parent family is no longer the status quo in America. So most readers will relate to these questions about step-parenting.]**

. . . I bury my face in my pillow as a rush of angry tears bubbles up from an untapped well within me. I wish I could cry prettily, but I have never been able to manage it. Hollywood actresses seem to weep effortlessly—tears flow from their mascaraed eyes and roll down perfectly sculpted cheeks. My tears spurt like geysers, accompanied by a red nose, a stuffy head, and labored breathing. In seconds I am such a sniffling, blubbering mess that I have to employ a dozen tissues to keep my airways clear. [**Again, every woman in the world will relate to this. Yes, she's crying and I'm describing it, but so realistically that every female reader understands. Not a whiff of sentimentality here.**]

Finally I fall back onto the bed, exhausted. I still don't have any answers, but at least I don't have to handle the shock of this discovery at home. Few people know me on St. Simons, so no one will care if I burst into tears in the middle of Fish Fever Lane or the Harris Teeter grocery store. Here I don't have to face my neighbors, my coworkers at church, or my friends. Here I won't have to face Michael . . . and I'll be able to process my thoughts without interference.

. . . As I close my eyes, a new thought strikes: for twenty-seven years, Michael and I have stopped what we were doing and headed to bed at eleven o'clock. I have drifted off to sleep with him by my side.

If he's gone . . . who's going to remind me to go to bed?[4] [**A thought shared by every divorced woman and widow. And notice the emotional shift—from angry and short in the beginning, to this self-pitying whisper.**]

One more scene, and this one is brief. From my book *The Novelist*, about a woman who's, well, a novelist. She is struggling with her young adult son, and in one scene she flashes back to a time when he was learning to walk:

When Zack was fourteen months old, he fell and hit his chin on the edge of a chair. I picked him up and wiped him off, but the sight of gaping flesh made me wince. I knew he'd need stitches. [**Every parent with a son will relate to this—**

it's a common accident with rambunctious little boys.]

I drove carefully to the emergency room, then held my baby on my lap as a doctor confirmed my suspicions. "Not a big deal," the physician told me. "Two stitches will do the trick." **[Notice the low "volume" of this scene. Despite the accident, everything is quiet and calm.]**

"Will it, you know, leave a scar?"

The doctor smiled. "Think of it as a badge of boyhood. I'll bet seventy percent of the men in this building have a similar scar on their chins. It's just one of those things." **[The reader is agreeing.]**

Zack, who had calmed by that time, seemed more intent on studying the stethoscope around the doctor's neck than in listening to this positive prognosis. **[A visual image all mothers of babies will remember from their own lives.]**

The nurse lifted Zack from my lap. He began to cry, stiffening his little body and reaching for me as the nurse wrestled him onto a papoose board. I stood and folded my arms, every nerve tensing as they restrained my son's arms and legs with wide Velcro bands. **[Many readers will recognize this sight or this helpless and frustrated feeling. Notice the folded arms— she has erected a wall between herself and what's happening on the exam table.]**

I bit my lip as my chin quivered. I've never been tied down like that, but I could imagine how helpless my little guy was feeling. The boy only had about ten words in his vocabulary, so he couldn't even verbalize his fears. **[Mom wants to cry, but doesn't dare. The audience supplies the missing emotion and concern.]**

I couldn't watch. I turned my head, studying a table loaded with medical instruments, as Zack shifted from screams to frenzied shrieks of the one word he had always used to summon help: "Ma-ma! Ma-ma! Ma-ma!"[5] [**Every mom or dad will relate to this frustrated reaction to the scream of a frightened child in pain. The volume has increased as well—from soft to screaming loud.**]

One book I found especially helpful when learning how to portray emotions was Ann Hood's *Creating Character Emotions*. The most important thing I learned while reading Hood's book is that emotions are not one-dimensional—strong feelings are almost always a blend of feelings. Anger, for instance, can be a blend of shock, anger, reproach, and helplessness. Shame can combine guilt, disgrace, embarrassment, and unworthiness. So if your character is in love, he may display signs of jealousy, sorrow, hope, desire, lust, fear, and even hate . . . sometimes in rapid succession.

Try to avoid having a character *tell* us what he's feeling—show us what he's feeling instead. We can't use photographs or drawings, but we have an entire dictionary of lovely words at our disposal, so go to it.

Body Language

I'm a sucker for body language books. Not only does a knowledge of body language allow me to entertain myself at parties, but it's an indispensable tool when I write.

In communication, only 7 percent of understanding derives from what is actually spoken. Thirty-eight percent comes from tone of voice, and a whopping 55 percent comes from the silent speech signals otherwise known as body language.

You should get a book on basic body language and memorize a few poses. Most you will translate instinctively. For instance, someone who stands with their arms folded across their chest is actually erecting a wall between himself and the outside world. Arms folded plus fists clenched may signify anger behind the wall.

One arm folded and one arm hanging down is what I consider the typical "middle school" pose. The person wants to be relaxed and accepted, but the other arm is in a defensive position just in case. At a glance, this person looks awkward and unsure.

Men who stand with their feet apart and thumbs tucked into belt or waistband, fingers pointing toward the crotch—well, if you think about it, that posture is self-explanatory. It's what I think of as *cowboy cocky*.

A woman who plays with her hair in the presence of a man is literally preening—she's attracted to the man. If she sits on the sofa with a foot tucked beneath her, her bent knee will most likely be pointed toward the man who has piqued her interest. If she kicks off her shoe while in this pose, well, she's *definitely* telegraphing her attraction to him.

A person who's insecure about a certain body part may touch it several times in the course of a situation—a bald man may rub his head, for example. A liar may tug on his ear or rub his nose. He may avoid direct eye contact, but other liars can look anyone in the eye and utter the boldest fabrications imaginable.

A boss who comes out from behind his desk and sits on the edge to look down at his employee may be subtly pointing out that he is *over* the employee. That he's a "bigger" man. Or woman, as the case may be.

The man or woman who touches your arm while you're talking is asking to cut into the conversation. You may be talking too much.

Body language is not an exact science—a girl may have her arms folded because she's cold—but it's useful to writers because if you use it in your dialogue and scenes, the reader will subconsciously pick up on these cues. So don't add body language merely as beats to break up extended passages of dialogue; make them count. Like this:

> Sylvia heard laughter from the next room. She had welcomed Charles and Melanie ten minutes before, and both said their respective spouses were on the way. "Harry always has to work late," Melanie had said, her lower lip protruding as she walked toward the living room, "but he'll make it."
>
> Sylvia put three glasses of iced tea on a tray and lifted it, then paused beneath the plastered archway. Charles and Melanie were both sitting on the sofa, but Charles was leaning away from Mel. Melanie had turned toward him, one elbow on the back of the sofa, the other playing with strands of

her long blonde hair. She flipped her hair over her shoulder and leaned toward Charles, forcing him to slant so far over the sofa's arm that Sylvia feared he might fall.

"Come on, Charlie," Melanie purred, apparently oblivious to Sylvia's presence. "Just give me your hand. I want to look at your lifeline, that's all."

Sylvia snorted beneath her breath. Poor old Harry couldn't arrive soon enough.

Sentiment versus Sentimentality

When a poem, song, or book is described as *sentimental*, it's not a compliment. The word usually describes something that goes after an emotional reaction without subtlety or finesse. The writer takes shortcuts and resorts to clichéd images. My dictionary says that a sentimental piece of literature, music, or art is "self-indulgent."

Some novelists are known for writing sentimental work. Their books can make me cry, too, but I hate myself for doing it. Shortcuts are fine if you only have three minutes for a music video, but novelists have no time constraint. We have hundreds of pages in which to establish genuine emotional content and context, so we have no reason to opt for sentimental shorthand.

For example: If you wanted to show how deeply a man loves his wife, what would you have him do? The lazy writer would have him bring home (I bet you've already supplied the answer) . . . a dozen red roses.

Fine, but how cliché is that?

In my book *The Fine Art of Insincerity*, the husband brings his wife a dozen red roses, but I turned the cliché on its head. Later my protagonist learns her husband is having a baby with another woman. She tells us:

> He has showered me with red roses . . . and
> every petal was a lie.

In your book, if you want to show how much a harried husband loves his wife, skip the roses and search for something unusual in the characters' backstory.

For instance, let's say Tom and Cathy have been married thirty years. They're like most long-married couples: comfortable with each other, but not exactly passionate. In an early chapter plant a brief mention of Cathy's childhood, months of which were spent on Clearwater Beach with her grandmother. Later have her reminisce about those sunny days and how much she loved that beach. Still later, have her find a picture of herself and her grandmother sitting in the sand with a beach bucket and shovel. Have Cathy brush away a tear while Tom silently looks on.

Then Cathy discovers a lump—and learns that she has breast cancer. Despite Tom's protests, she worries that he won't find her desirable any more. She is no longer young, she's put on a few pounds, and all day Tom is surrounded by young and pretty women at the Honda dealership where he works.

Later, when she awakens from a successful mastectomy, have Tom *not* be by her side. How does she react? With despair? Anger? Grief? Does his absence confirm her fears about no longer being desirable and beautiful?

But then Tom rushes in with a big bag in his hand. When she asks what he's carrying, he sheepishly pulls out the photo of her and Grandma, now freshly restored. He sets it on the hospital bed table, then creates a tableau of plastic beach bucket, shovel, and a small plastic bag of white sand, tied at the top with a ribbon stamped *Wish you could be in Clearwater Beach.*

Clearly, the man has gone to great lengths to make her happy.

Cathy struggles to restrain her tears, but she reaches out to him and he gently takes her in his arms.

That's how you depict love. And if you want to practice what you're learning here, choose a scene from the above storyline and write it up—perhaps the scene where Cathy learns that her breast lump was a malignant cancer. Try to incorporate as many emotion-evoking methods as you can.

How'd you do?

In Summation
Use your characters' qualities and histories to create three-dimensional scenes, and write with your readers' emotions and memories in mind.

Establishing honest sentiment is a lot harder than tossing in a dash of clichéd sentimentality, but if you are writing the Tom and Cathy story, your reader will never look at a plastic beach bucket without thinking of your characters.

Never go for the obvious. Work hard to think of something unexpected.

Not everyone cries as easily as I do, but it never hurts to weep while you write. Robert Frost said, "No tears in the writer, no tears in the reader. No surprise in the writer, no surprise in the reader."

Dig deep into *your* emotional well when you write. Call up the emotions you felt when you got married, when your first child was born, when you lost your job, when you were betrayed, when you lost someone you loved.

Once you've called up those feelings, don't just write, "I felt sad. Really sad." Instead, depict your sadness in a fresh way, using language that's sharp and clear and clean.

Look for metaphors that illustrate how something feels through comparison: An empty house paired with a death in the family. A gap in the line of Christmas stockings on the mantle paired with an estranged son no one ever mentions. A skittish stray dog paired with a foster child who has been abused.

If you feel emotion as you write, your reader will, too.

The average person might find this odd, but every time tragedy strikes my family, I find my fingers itching for paper and pen even as my brain tries to cope with the situation. I want to write down everything I'm feeling, every single emotion, because some day I will use it. I want to record concrete details—what things looked and smelled like, how my stomach turned over, or how my fingers tingled as a rush of adrenaline ebbed away.

As a firm believer in the providence of God, I believe everything happens for a reason. And because I'm a writer, everything is fodder for my life in pages.

So start keeping a journal. You can write in it every day if you like, but I'd rather you reach for it when you're feeling great emotions. Record those impressions, feelings, insights, and physical reactions. One day you will use them.

Are you ready? If you've read the **Writing Lessons from the Front** in order, you should have a skeleton for your plot, a cast of terrific characters, a point of view established, and a plan for revising your manuscript. Now, during revision, you will be able to make sure your scenes evoke the emotion you want the reader to experience. I hope you're willing to do this important work . . . because that's the entire purpose of an novel.

Remember what Sol Stein said? The novelist's primary job is to *create an emotional experience for the reader.*

I've created a checklist to help you make sure you use every tool at your disposal. Feel free to copy it for your own use but please don't mass produce and pass it out at conferences and meetings.

These books are brief for a reason, you know—I don't want you to spend most of your time reading how-to books. I want you to spend most of your time writing, Put what you've learned into practice. *That's* the best way to improve.

So go ahead—get back to work on your manuscript and make it the best it can be. The world is waiting to laugh and cry with your characters.

Evoking Emotion Checklist

Overall considerations:

1. Do you have scenes or a story line intended to evoke laughter or smiles from your reader?

2. Do you have lots of sensory detail in your most emotional scenes? Things your character sees, smells, feels, hears, and/or tastes?

3. Have you made certain to fully develop your protagonist's emotional reactions at key moments of the book? For instance, if something traumatic happens to your hero, have you jumped to another event without letting the reader experience your hero's reaction? Have you short-changed the reader at key emotional moments?

Scene-specific considerations:

4. In a particular emotional scene, have you reached for the clichéd symbol or have you taken the time to imbue something else with great meaning?

5. Have you kept in mind that many emotions are mixed with other emotions? What is the chief emotion your character feels in this scene? _____ What other feelings are mixed with this one? _____

6. What sort of personal emotional memories will your reader think of when he or she reads this scene? What stage of life is your likely reader in? Childhood? Young adulthood? Young parent? Middle aged parent? Senior adult? Give your reader's probable life experiences, how can you write or edit this scene to better tap into your reader's emotional memory? What images can you include? What sounds? Smells? Sensations?

7. What is present in the scene (landscape, weather, furnishings, background noise) that could provide "mood music" in the background of this scene? Write it in at appropriate places.

8. How does the volume of this scene change? If this is a "loud" scene, would it be more effective if you brought the volume down to a whisper?

Does the scene start softly and end with a bang? Does it start soft, become loud, and return to a quiet ending? If it were a musical piece, what sort of piece would it be?

Is the scene all on one level? Find a way to either ratchet up the volume or tone it down as the scene draws to a close.

9. How does dialogue enhance the emotional impact of this scene? Should your characters say more or less? Should their voices crack with grief or laughter? Should they be direct, or should they take pains to talk about everything but the one topic uppermost in their minds?

Is their body language appropriate for what they are thinking and feeling in this scene? What are they communicating through their body language?

10. Could memories enhance the emotional impact of this scene? Could your protagonist or point of view character have a memory flash through his mind? (But try to avoid flashbacks in the first chapters of the book. That's where you want to focus on moving forward.)

11. Who will be the most emotionally affected by this scene? To whom is the reader most closely bonded? Is this the best point of view character for this scene? Would the scene be more or less moving if events were recorded from someone else's perspective?

Notes:

Thank you for purchasing this book in **Writing Lessons from the Front.** If you find any typos in this book, please write and let us know: hunthaven@gmail.com.

We would also appreciate it if you would be kind enough to leave a review of this book on Amazon. Thank you!

Writing Lessons from the Front:

1. **The Plot Skeleton**
2. **Creating Extraordinary Characters**
3. **Point of View**
4. **Tracking Down the Weasel Words**
5. **Evoking Emotion**
6. **Write Your Book: Process and Planning**

ABOUT THE AUTHOR

Angela Hunt writes for readers who have learned to expect the unexpected from this versatile writer. With over four million copies of her books sold worldwide, she is the best-selling author of more than 120 works ranging from picture books (*The Tale of Three Trees*) to novels and nonfiction.

Now that her two children have reached their twenties, Angie and her husband live in Florida with Very Big Dogs (a direct result of watching *Turner and Hooch* too many times). This affinity for mastiffs has not been without its rewards—one of their dogs was featured on *Live with Regis and Kelly* as the second-largest canine in America. Their dog received this dubious honor after an all-expenses-paid trip to Manhattan for the dog and the Hunts, complete with VIP air travel and a stretch limo in which they toured New York City. Afterward, the dog gave out pawtographs at the airport.

Angela admits to being fascinated by animals, medicine, unexplained phenomena, and "just about everything." Books, she says, have always shaped her life— in the fifth grade she learned how to flirt from reading *Gone with the Wind.*

Her books have won the coveted Christy Award, several Angel Awards from Excellence in Media, and the Gold and Silver Medallions from *Foreword Magazine*'s Book of the Year Award. In 2007, her novel *The Note* was featured as a Christmas movie on the Hallmark channel. She recently completed her doctorate in biblical literature and is now finishing her doctorate in Theology.

When she's not home writing, Angie often travels to teach writing workshops at schools and writers' conferences. And to talk about her dogs, of course. Readers may visit her web site at www.angelahuntbooks.com.

Selected Novels by Angela Hunt

The Offering
The Fine Art of Insincerity
Five Miles South of Peculiar
The Face
Let Darkness Come
The Elevator
The Novelist
The Awakening
The Truth Teller
Unspoken
Uncharted
The Justice
The Canopy
The Immortal
Doesn't She Look Natural ?
She Always Wore Red
She's In a Better Place
The Pearl
The Note
The Debt
Then Comes Marriage
The Shadow Women
Dreamers
Brothers
Journey
Roanoke
Jamestown
Hartford
Rehoboth
Charles Towne
The Proposal
The Silver Sword
The Golden Cross
The Velvet Shadow
The Emerald Isle

ENDNOTES

[1] Sol Stein, *Stein on Writing* (New York: St. Martin's Press, 1995), p. 8.

[2] E.L. Doctorow quoted in Sol Stein's *Stein on Writing*, ibid.

[3] Angela Hunt, *Unspoken* (Nashville, TN: Thomas Nelson, 2005).

[4] Angela Hunt, *The Fine Art of Insincerity* (Nashville, TN: Howard Publishing, 2011).

[5] Angela Hunt, *The Novelist* (Nashville, TN: Thomas Nelson, 2006).